Still Life

the Art of Nurturing a Tranquil Soul

Still Life

the Art of Nurturing a Tranquil Soul

Mary Jenson

MULTNOMAH PUBLISHERS

Sisters, Oregon

STILL LIFE

published by Multnomah Publishers, Inc.

© 1997 by Mary Jenson

International Standard Book Number: 1-57673-145-6

Cover illustration by Martha Alf
Cover design by Jeff Gelfuso

Printed in the United States of America

Scripture quotations are from:
The Holy Bible, New International Version (NIV)
© 1973, 1984 by International Bible Society,
used by permission of Zondervan Publishing House

For information:
MULTNOMAH PUBLISHERS, INC.
POST OFFICE BOX 1720
SISTERS, OREGON 97759

Library of Congress Cataloging-in-Publication Data
Jenson, Mary E. Still life: the art of nurturing a tranquil soul/by Mary Jenson
p.cm.   Includes index.   ISBN 1-57673-145-6 (alk. paper)
1. Peace of mind--Religious aspects--Christianity.   I. Title.
BV4908.5.J46   1997   242--dc21   97-20973   CIP

97 98 99 00 01 02 03 04 — 10 9 8 7 6 5 4 3 2 1

To the memory of my parents
and the company of my sisters

Still Life

the Art of Nurturing a Tranquil Soul

Acknowledgments

Thank you to Heather Harpham Kopp
and Carol Bartley, my editors.
Without you, this book would be a tangled mess.
Really.

One Small Stone

One

One Small Stone

RELEARNING SIMPLICITY

It was a chilly, cloudy day. My husband, Ron, and I walked the tree-lined path around a small lake. We found ourselves alone—except for a solitary fisherman who took our picture for us on the shore of the famous pond. We didn't talk much. The stillness was real, palpable. Eventually we came upon the rubble of a cottage where a pensive young man once wrote: "I went to the woods because I wished to live deliberately...."

People from all over the world add small stones to the rubble at

Walden Pond in honor of Henry David Thoreau. His ruminations on nature and a tranquil lifestyle have likewise fascinated Ron and me for years. So when we saw the Walden sign, on our twenty-fifth anniversary trip near Boston, we had to stop for a visit.

Before we left, I added a stone of my own to the cottage's memorial pile.

Something about this peaceful, reverent place reawakened a deep-seated desire in me. I too want to live deliberately. To pare down and throw out. To make do with essentials instead of continually smothering those essentials with commercials.

As we left Walden Pond, I wistfully asked Ron, "Could we sell our home and buy a pond?"

Thoreau would have understood. He said himself, "I wanted to live deep and suck out all the marrow of life, to live so sturdily and Spartan-like as to put to rout all that was not life, to cut a broad swath and shave close, to drive life into a corner, and reduce it to its lowest terms...."[1]

I'm probably not ready to "put to rout all that is not life," but I'm close to being ready to "drive life into a corner."

I long for a more tranquil life.

I've yearned for my own Walden Pond at times, particularly when my children were young. While I was in the middle of sweeping up Cheerios and dog hair, and cutting peanut butter sandwiches into squares, I would dream about the more serene life I'd have someday when my kids were older—or even grown.

These days my son, Matt, is in college. His room is as neat as an accountant's office. No clothes on the floor, no comforter in a wad, no jazz on the stereo. Though we talk often, I don't remember *exactly* what his hands look like, feel like. I'm starved for the touch of his skin.

And my daughter, Molly, (her room is not neat!) is a teenager with wheels, off to college next fall. (Believe me, I'm studying every inch of her hands.) Quiet is plentiful these days. And space. I thought the space and quiet would bring a still life. Not in the manner of being "unmoving" or "motionless," but in the way so many of us are looking for: calm, tranquil, serene. Now I'm surprised to find that something is still missing…

For many years I've been drawn to still-life paintings for the same reason I'm drawn to Walden Pond. The paintings themselves speak to me about tranquillity. So much so, I can't help wondering: What if I were to examine my life in light of the elements that make a still-life painting so serene, so appealing? Things like simplicity of subject, the appreciation of the ordinary, light and shadow, color, lots of space?

I've discovered that a reference point, especially a unique and compelling one, can help me see my life anew. If all I can see is what's around me, I get overwhelmed by a stack of bills, my husband's books occupying every flat surface, the streaks on my windows, Molly's latest shopping trip flung across the furniture.

But when I consider a still-life painting I love—like the solitary pears on the cover of this book—the beauty speaks to me. Of singleness of heart. Of peace. Of simplicity. I want to learn how to take such elements and make them a part of my inner life. And I'd like it if that inner life would spill over to the outer one as well.

In a world of cell phones, express lanes, call waiting, and kids with schedules that would challenge an executive, we struggle to find a quiet, spiritual center. And even more so to understand what God means when He says, "Be still…"

Stillness must be something deeper, more subtle, more encompassing than I previously thought. It must center more on inner sources and less on outer ones. It must not be dependent upon care-free circumstances, serene surroundings, or lack of children underfoot. It's not even a product of quiet or inactivity.

In fact, we have to be able to find it in the middle of chaos. Few of us can drop our lives in midair and move to a pond. But maybe we can learn from artists like Martha Alf, who created the art on the cover, and from pioneers like Thoreau. We can start at the same place I think they did—by making radical choices in favor of simplicity.

The very possibility makes my soul salivate. I'm ready to make radical choices too.

❧

Simplicity is one of the first things we notice about still-life art. With some exceptions, most still lifes use only a few isolated objects. A jug and a loaf of bread. Pears on a counter. Spartan choices that say as much about what was left out as what was put in.

Surely, what simplicity does for a painting—establishes a sense of order, of stillness, peace, and purity—it can also do for our harried souls.

We all agree: We want to worry about less. We want to feel clean, purified, at peace inside. We want order without and calm within. But so often our attempts at simplicity go awry. Or nowhere. Or get lost in a pile.

Is there any woman who doesn't feel this need keenly almost every day? When it gets too strong, I usually start cleaning. The clutter around me reminds me of the clutter within. So I attack the garage, the Tupperware collection, the junk drawer in the kitchen. I even throw out superfluous cosmetics I'm convinced I'll need someday…

But a month later the spaces are filled again. With that kind of turnaround, what chance do any of us have, even if we *find* simplicity, to hold on to it?

Recently I read about a woman who lived with two Amish families for a number of weeks in her search to define simplicity in her life. She participated in their simple lifestyle and went without such amenities as electric lights and a car. She found a level of peaceful existence in the Amish model—routine schedules, unhurried service, unadorned and uncluttered homes.

But surely God does not intend for us to unearth our long skirts from the seventies and move to the Amish country, does He?

I have no intention of making that kind of move, nor of pruning my possessions down to the barely there. Yet I like the idea of purging my life of much of the unnecessary—if it kills me. Or maybe I'll keep the absolutely necessary and the moderately necessary, and throw out the slightly necessary. Or…keep the slightly necessary and throw out just the frills. Except those are the things I love…

Oh, rats. Forget the whole mess!

❧

Painting a still life is like living in Amish country. You have to pare away all but the essentials. That isn't as simple as it seems, however. An artist has a vast array of options before her—subject, colors, shadows, composition. She must make hard choices, direct the viewer's focus, and convey a single theme or intent through her art.

Like the artist, most of us encounter daily such a vast array of options it boggles the mind—and jumbles the soul. Our choices range from what kind of soap to buy, to what to wear to lunch, to what make of car to rent while ours is in the shop (but which shop to use?). These choices are a blessing, on the one hand. But they can also clutter up our lives.

Sue Bender, the woman who visited the Amish, writes, "Before I went to the Amish, I thought that the more choices I had, the luckier I'd be. But there is a big difference between having many choices and making a choice. Making a choice—declaring what is essential—creates a framework for a life that eliminates many choices but gives meaning to the things that remain."[2]

Anne Lindbergh, wife of aviator Charles Lindbergh and mother of five, put it this way, "One cannot collect all the beautiful shells on the beach. One can collect only a few, and they are more beautiful if they are a few. One moon shell is more impressive than three. There is only one moon in the sky. One double-sunrise is an event; six are a succession, like a week of school days. Gradually one discards and keeps just the perfect specimen; not necessarily a rare shell, but a perfect one of its kind."[3]

Where is that one shell? What is important? What is trivial? What do I ultimately want to lay claim to at the cost of other things? Asking isn't enough. Making choices—giving up one thing in favor of another—is how I begin to create a framework for simplicity. And that takes focus.

Focus is deliberate, targeted contemplation. It is the opposite of distraction. It means that we are bringing all of our intellectual attention to bear on one thing we've chosen. On one perfect shell. Or on one aspect of a not-so-perfect life.

Today I'm looking for focus at Lake Hodges, which is only five minutes away. It's about as different from Walden Pond as another contained body of water could be. It's huge and stretches out in several directions like a glove made for an oddly shaped hand. The banks rise up to good-sized hills in some places, flat grassland in others.

My plan is to take out a small motorboat all by myself. I walk down the pier with a satchel over my shoulder as if this is what I always do on Wednesdays. I feel brave and strong—no one but me knows I've tucked a cellular phone in my bag just in case.

I back slowly out of the slip. It takes a few minutes every time to get reaccustomed to moving the tiller the right way. (My friend Bruce can maneuver a sixty-foot sailboat into a sixty-three-foot parallel parking space with no trouble at all. I struggle with my eight-foot motorboat and a direct shot into a slip twice its size.)

Whenever I'm out on the lake, everything seems simpler. The clutter in my garage is far enough away as to be nearly irrelevant; the decisions I have to make lose their immediacy; I could make some phone calls on my cell phone, but I pretend that's impossible.

Here in a boat in this calm water it's easy to dismiss the extraneous. The quiet and the solitude allow me the focus I need. I suspect we could live very simple lives in Thoreau's cabin if no one knew we were there (or was allowed in). It's easy to focus if there's nothing to disturb or distract.

But as I learned the day Matt was born, even when focus is absolutely necessary, it's still hard to maintain. I'd missed the child-birth class when they took the tour of the labor room, and though Ron would be with me soon, he wasn't allowed in until the nurses were good and ready to let him. These days it's not so, but that labor room was sterile and cold, and I was scared to death.

And lonely. We'd had constant reminders during our classes that the mother-to-be was to focus her mind away from the discomfort (they wouldn't let us call it pain) and onto music, or a painting on the wall, or even a flower on the wallpaper. The longer I was without my husband/coach, the stronger the pull to give in to the disturbing thoughts that filled my mind. My focus was right where it *wasn't* supposed to be, and my body was tensing up like an overblown balloon, an object I resembled to a large extent.

When Ron came in, he brought a book—not a good sign. And he and my doctor were friends. So here I was, lying on the table, nearing transition, with the fetal monitor pressing like Chinese torture on one tender spot on my tummy. I was trying to focus on a particular spot of wallpaper and not on this most amazing and painful thing happening to my body. And Ron and Don were standing over me, having a great conversation complete with jokes and laughter.

You can imagine what happened to my focus. The more distracted I became, the more uncomfortable I grew. Finally, I gave up on focusing and lost the benefits of calm and tranquillity my teachers promised would be there.

Even when our whole focus is on focusing, it's hard to do. No wonder it seems impossible when we're distracted by life at every turn. We settle down for a quiet moment, and the phone rings. We set aside a weekend to clean out the closets, and our best friend gets pneumonia and we need to watch her toddlers and get her firstborn to soccer practice.

Is there a way to focus in the middle of it all? Do we have to lose our focus with each distraction that comes along? The ability to focus cannot merely mean being able to grit our teeth and keep our eyes on one piece of wallpaper, can it?

❧

Out on Lake Hodges, there are only a few places to go. Although it's a big lake, I can cover it in an hour if I keep moving. I can carry only a small number of things with me, and these I choose carefully—something to read or study, something to snack on, a blanket to use as cover or cushion.

My little boat putt-putts noisily between the buoys. Now and then I see a splash out of the corner of my eyes—a fish jumping toward a miniature meal. I watch slender egrets take flight like lanky athletes rising in a pole vault. They have not much on their minds—food, shelter, nesting babies. I envy their grace, their flight, their singleness of being.

Funny, I think. Most of what I have on *my* mind is food, shelter, and "nesting babies" too. But the choices, the maintenance, the requests! Would that I could live at Lake Hodges like the egrets and limit the choices of my mind and the confusion in my soul.

And really, that's the question here. How can I nurture a tranquil soul with so many things vying for my time?

The ancient religious fathers knew that the key to tranquillity was the simplicity of wanting and needing one thing—God. They were serious about the simple. And it makes me wonder, just how serious am I about wanting a still life? Am I serious enough to will and to want *one* thing—and that thing to be Christ? Am I willing for Him to be my focus?

Sören Kierkegaard wrote a book with an intriguing title: *Purity of Heart Is to Will One Thing*. Professor Dallas Willard says, "The person who has grown to the place where he or she can truly say with Paul, 'This one thing I do' (Philippians 3:13), or who truly 'seeks first the kingdom of God and His righteousness' (Matthew 6:33), is a person who has entered into simplicity."[4] This is the central call of the Christian life. God and His kingdom is the one thing to "will."

Several days ago "willing one thing" became plate-glass clear in my mind. I was driving up the hill with a screaming ambulance on my tail. We stopped at the same place—my house!—where I found my neighbors and Molly standing over Ron, who had passed out in a chair.

Nothing we did could wake him, although he seemed to be sleeping peacefully. Molly and I sat by his side in the emergency room until he finally "woke up" after three hours, healthy but groggy. Later we determined he'd had an adverse reaction to some allergy medicine.

From the moment I saw Ron unconscious until he walked unassisted out of the hospital to the car, I was *very* conscious of God. And I willed one thing. It went beyond Ron's health, beyond my future, beyond Molly's security. It was only God. I willed God. I prayed our needs, but I willed God's will.

In the middle of its raw moments, life becomes very simple. We find out then what's of primary importance, and we discover our resources—where and what they are and whether they'll hold us up. The more we "will one thing," and that thing is God and His will, the "stiller" our lives will be. And the simpler!

❧

I don't suppose I'll ever think of simplicity without wanting to straighten some clutter somewhere. But that's all right.

"The Christian Discipline of simplicity is an inward reality that results in an outward life-style," writes Richard Foster. "Both the inward and outward aspects of simplicity are essential. We deceive ourselves if we believe we can possess the inward reality without its having a profound effect on how we live. To attempt to arrange an outward life-style of simplicity without the inward reality leads to deadly legalism."[5]

Of course I'll spring-clean and weed out the extraneous stuff from my home. Periodically I'll evaluate the activities that compete for my precious time. All that's well and good. "We are not trying to get out of the pain and pressure of contemporary living," Calvin Miller reminds us. "We are simply taking steps to infuse it with meaning."[6]

I think I'm getting it now. At first we *want* simplicity, so we clean the house. But finally, we clean the house because we've *found* simplicity inside.

∽

I turn my little boat toward the dock and rehearse in my mind the exact moment I need to kill the motor so it will drift gently into the slip. The sun's at my back—the same back that is cramped by having to twist around to operate the steering. Lake Hodges is calm; the egrets have settled somewhere I cannot see. My heart is still.

In a sense I've been in my own still-life painting. A few objects—a boat, a blanket, a book. A simple background—blue sky, shimmering lake, gorse-covered hills.

As I step out of the rocking boat, I'm reminded that while I can't carry Lake Hodges with me (or Walden Pond, for that matter), I can hold on to the peace in my soul. It doesn't come from water and egrets and bobbing boats; it comes from the inside, from the One who never changes.

I pull up in my driveway and walk into a house full of piles—of laundry next to the washer, of mail on the kitchen counter, of phone calls backed up on my machine. In one of my kitchen cupboards, all my spices are in a jumbled mess, the result of a frustrated attempt to find some vanilla.

Simplicity may not have a measurable effect on our kitchen cupboards. But it will always exert enormous influence on the panorama of our lives—our choices of time and priorities and focus. When God's will becomes the center of our lives, all our choices seem to line up, unbidden, in order before Him.

"It is to the extent that we worship Him, and surrender our lives to Him, and are led by Him, that His kingdom comes in our hearts."[7] That sounds like a tall order, but it's really pretty simple.

White Time

Two

White Time

CREATING MARGINS OF QUIET SPACE

Daylight savings time ended this past weekend. It's light at 5:30 in the morning now, but not at 5:30 in the evening, and much easier to think about getting out of bed. The coffee's delicious. I warm my hands on the curved ceramic, holding the cup as if it's a pint of blood about to give me life.

My husband's up even earlier than I am—but he's downstairs in his office. My daughter sleeps till the last possible minute. Breakfast can wait for now.

Out my window, the sky is clear except for a long bank of puffy clouds in the east. As the sun rises, I watch them change from soft pink to brilliant magenta. Is anyone else seeing this? I am about to call down to Ron's office to tell him to look when I hear him open the sliding door.

I love this quiet time of morning, this white space. It's one of the margins[1] of my life that gives me strength.

Priest Henri Nouwen would call it "desert time." In his book *The Way of the Heart* he describes the experiences with solitude, silence, and prayer of the fourth- and fifth-century Egyptian Desert Fathers. He urges us, "Precisely because our secular milieu offers us so few spiritual disciplines, we have to develop our own. We have, indeed, to fashion our own desert where we can withdraw every day, shake off our compulsions, and dwell in the gentle healing presence of our Lord."[2]

❧

As our own lives need the desert, so still-life paintings rely a great deal on what's called "negative space," the areas around the subjects. Unoccupied spaces are as carefully planned as the arrangement of the objects. A "busy" composition calls for a simple background. In fact, if there's too much going on in the space behind the subjects, can we really "see" the flowers or the fruit?

Similarly, God has given each of us a need for space—room to think, to evaluate, to dream. And when we're fortunate or determined enough to find that solitude, that white time, it changes us. Truths we need to remember are brought to the forefront, and our attention is drawn to the things that really matter.

Anne Lindbergh wrote about space in *Gift from the Sea*. She said, "For it is only framed in space that beauty blooms. Only in space are events and objects and people unique and significant—and therefore beautiful. A tree has significance if one sees it against the empty face of sky. A note in music gains significance from the silences on either side. A candle flowers in the space of night. Even small and casual things take on significance if they are washed in space, like a few autumn grasses in one corner of an Oriental painting, the rest of the page bare."[3]

I think of an oil painting called "Still Life with a White Mug"[4] which uses a completely neutral background to set off two pears, three apples, a knife, and a mug sitting on a thick wood table. Because the space is so plain and plentiful, the beauty of the subjects themselves is brought forward and made clear.

So it is with us. Space brings peace, beauty, and clarity. Just as we appreciate books with margins enough to rest and refocus our eyes, so we long for margins in our lives to rest and refocus everything else. But how do we create that uninterrupted white time?

Not long ago I was reminded how hard it is to protect our structured time much less to find and protect spare minutes for ourselves.

The day started off well enough. I got my walk and my shower, unloaded the dishwasher, and cleaned the refrigerator—all before 9:30. I was on a roll. It was going to be a productive writing day. I could feel it.

Then the phone rang. I decided to answer it, since there was no need to screen my calls yet.

My seventeen-year-old daughter was calling from school. "Mom, can I come home? I feel *so* sick." Okay, she's on her way. That's all right. She'll probably sleep. God knows what I need to get done today, and He'd want me to put my family first.

I sit at my computer. The phone again. Well, just one more answer.

"Mom?" My son in college. "Could you go through all my files, find the notes from Dr. Holmes's class, and read them to me over the phone?"

"Sure, Matt." I find his papers, call him back, and convince him overnight mail would be more efficient.

"I love you, Mom."

"Me too, honey."

Back to the computer.

"Mom?"

"What, Molly?"

"I'm supposed to hand in the money for my school pictures today at lunch. I just feel so sick. Do I have a fever?"

"I don't think so, honey. Let's take your temperature. Now when does lunch start? And where do I go?"

I drive to school and glare at a van going under the speed limit.

Back to my computer.

"Mom?"

"Yes, honey."

"I'm really hungry. Could you make me some lunch?"

"Sure, babe. Soup sound good?"

"Mmmm."

Nearly every woman I know has had a day, or many, like that one. Our lives are so punctuated by interruptions that periodically we need to pull away, like Jesus, and go off by ourselves to find a quiet space.

Sometimes finding space is the only way we can see ourselves as distinct from the others who surround us. As a young mother, I often felt in danger of getting lost in the background of my own life, of being described only in terms of my family. With much of my focus on my husband and children (and rightly so), it was too easy not to attend to my own self.

When my husband noticed me slowly going stir-crazy, he was understanding and enlightened enough to suggest I go away for a weekend alone. I took him up on it. I slept, planned, prayed, and ate entire meals without one glass of spilled milk, one argument, or one comment on the quality of the food. Those occasional retreats, when my children were small, began the jealous guardianship of my solitude.

Anne Lindbergh also took retreats, and wrote the following while at the beach: "My life in Connecticut, I begin to realize, lacks this quality of significance and therefore of beauty, because there is so little empty space. The space is scribbled on; the time has been filled. There are so few empty pages in my engagement pad, or empty hours in the day, or empty rooms in my life in which to stand alone and find myself."[5]

Solitude isn't reserved for women with housekeepers and time on their hands though. Space of our own is something we all need. Susanna Wesley, who had eighteen children, found space behind her apron. When she wanted to get away, she'd throw her apron up over her head. That signaled her children to be quiet and leave her alone. (Of course the amount of thinking that can happen in a week at the beach probably can't happen in a few minutes behind an apron!)

My friend Glenda has carved out a nice little piece of solitude. Her husband has graciously agreed to get their two girls ready for and off to school Mondays, Wednesdays, and Fridays. On those days, Glenda leaves her house at 5:30 for a workout swim, then hits Starbucks for coffee, and hunkers down in her car in the corner of a parking lot for her own period of solitude.

I couldn't have done that when my kids were younger. Even early morning walks were not in the picture. Ron wasn't available and I needed my sleep! I stole time alone during my children's naps, on Saturdays when Ron was around, and, finally, with Ron's blessing, on weekends away by myself.

Now I find it on my walks with Homer—our mutt with the human eyes—and in the still moments of the morning before the chaos hits. I find it on the freeway with classical music on the radio, or with no music at all. Sometimes I find it at Lake Hodges or in my backyard hammock. We women have to be creative. Five minutes of space in the bathroom will have to do some days; other times we might really get to run away to another place and think until we're bored.

ৡ

Today I set out the door with Homer at 7:30. It's brisk and clear. The sun's had two hours of workout time and is doing a pretty good job of warming up the morning. Homer's frisky. I let him stop when he needs to but encourage him to keep moving after the eighteenth leg lift. It's a quiet morning. I strain to hear only nature.

The leaves are falling. No autumn color to speak of, but every now and then a satisfying crunch under my feet. I look up at the sky.

Clouds are forming; we're supposed to have rain tonight.

The sky is never empty, I've read, even if it's blue and clear. In an ounce of air there are a thousand billion trillion molecules of oxygen and nitrogen. Really. Nor is the cliché "as light as air" even remotely true. Our atmosphere weighs 5,000 trillion tons. Only a force as relentless and unforgiving as gravity could hold it to earth.

As empty as the sky can look, it isn't.

❧

…And neither is my mind. Even a mother with nearly grown children and a clean house can have a head full of clutter. With so many issues demanding attention, I realize even more sharply that purely physical space doesn't guarantee mental margins. We can be on a Maui beach all by ourselves and, without realizing it, let our thoughts spin on that same hamster wheel we thought we'd left behind.

The conflict between the trivial and the grand is where I battle—beach or not. I sit down to write, to imagine, to ponder—and wind up thinking about dinner or remembering the phone calls I need to return. It's frustrating to be looking for the meditative, the contemplative, the poetic—and end up with the mundane. (I drift along/unsure of my going/a tiny spider in the wind/don't forget bread and dog food.)

But how do we go about creating mental margins? Is there some place in our brains that we can selectively erase, like the part that remembers our old phone number or the name of our sixth-grade teacher? Then maybe we could hold more tenaciously onto important thoughts and memories, like the progression of a deep, theological answer to the problems of the world. Or the last conversation we had with our college student.

There's the rub, that's the trick—exchanging the unimportant for the images, words, and thoughts that frame, feed, and tame our souls. The art is not only in the emptying but also in the filling.

Calvin Miller says, "There's some force in the universe that doesn't like empty boxes! So when the emptiness is not filled by careful design, it becomes a catchall. The box is a parable of Christians in our time. Designed to bear the power of God, we are haphazardly filled with the trivia of our world."[6]

White space must be filled with *something*. It can't stay pristine, untouched, but for a moment. Our minds are never empty—like the sky is not empty. They're filled with what we allow in there. Space and solitude give us the chance to brush away the trivia and fill our minds with thoughts that feed us like a banquet.

Philippians 4:8 says, "Finally, brothers, whatever is true, whatever is noble, whatever is right, whatever is pure, whatever is lovely, whatever is admirable—if anything is excellent or praiseworthy—think about such things."

❧

"Thinking about such things" was not the initial goal of my white time. But as in many areas of our lives, we can start out with one goal and find a more important one en route. It wasn't until I found some space for myself that I began to realize the true value of solitude.

"We say to each other that we need some solitude in our lives," writes Nouwen. "What we really are thinking of, however, is a time and a place for ourselves in which we are not bothered by other people…. For us, solitude most often means privacy…a place where we gather new strength to continue the ongoing competition in life…."

Privacy is not an invalid destination; we need it on a regular basis. Sometimes all I did on my weekends away was pamper myself. But Nouwen goes on to say, "Solitude is not a private therapeutic place.

Rather, it is the place of conversion, the place where the old self dies and the new self is born, the place where the emergence of the new man and the new woman occurs."[7]

When we're fortunate enough to have time alone, how wonderful to use a good deal of it for regeneration, rebirth, and "emergence." We make the best use of solitude, of white time, when we empty ourselves of our props—our books, our TV Guides, our lists and goals—and fill ourselves with God. In God's presence we can stand exposed yet safe. There we are most fully ourselves. There we can address our deepest longings, inadequacies, and needs. He is the Maker. There we can be remade into the image of His Son.

(Oh, I think to myself, I'm slogging through holy ground in oversized boots, leaving prints as big as potholes.)

What we learn in times of solitude is what we need in times of chaos. The more we read about who God is and what He says, the easier it is to trust Him and find Him in our day-to-day lives. The more we pray and listen to God in our white times, the easier it is to hear Him when we are fragmented and distracted. "The more we train ourselves to spend time with God and him alone," says Henri Nouwen, "the more we will discover that God is with us at all times and in all places. Then we will be able to recognize him even in the midst of a busy and active life."[8]

We won't see Him just in the crises, but also in the happy moments, in the serendipitous events, in the minor—and major—frustrations. Just yesterday, in fact, I was typing away with great genius and speed—every word, every sentence perfect—and my computer crashed. I lost it all, and by the time my tantrum was over, I'd lost the ideas as well. What can the world give me when, as in this case, retrieval is impossible? Nothing. What can God give me? Peace…patience…the freedom to cry and rant and rave…and the assurance that He cares. It's in solitude that we come to know the God who is as present in our daily frustrations as in our times of worship.

This morning, after reading in Psalm 50 that God desires a sacrifice of thanksgiving, I do that throughout my walk. I make a point to distinguish the many shades of green I see, and to notice what's happening to all the trees this early fall. I think through the people I'm committed to pray for—but today turn my pleas for God's intervention into expectant words of gratitude for His answers.

I'm learning to release God from the confines of smallness, to let Him overpower the fixed, hampered shadow of the Being I'm inclined to make Him into. How we impede His glory (He lets us, you know) when we demote Him to a stereotype or even to a description! When we limit Him by ignorance or neglect, we relegate Him to Someone out there. We hold Him at arm's length, and we segregate Him from our daily lives.

God could have chosen to be known in a minute, with no effort on our part at all. Instead, He wants us to break a little sweat and search for Him with all our hearts. He promised we could find Him. I don't want to give up until I find Him all.

These simple walks, small margins of time set aside for myself and God alone (and Homer, but he doesn't count), show me that solitude is not for running *away* but for running *to*. It's not for emptying my mind, my time, but for filling it with the right food, with the nourishment that comes from opening myself to the fact that God is around me and with me and listening to me. When I run to that place of quiet, I find perspective and peace. Then I'm ready to meet the world.

Homer and I round the corner for home. From that spot I have a nearly unobstructed view of the sky and the surrounding horizon where it touches down. It's an overwhelming sight. The space is filled with clouds, the diaphanous breaths of God. They're so magnificent I pay too much attention to them and nearly send both Homer and myself sprawling in the street just to get a good look.

Underneath this borderless still life of sky and clouds, I am awed by the space I see and feel. God is both out there and in me. Far from feeling lost in such vastness, I feel surrounded by God, filled by Him. I am His and I am becoming like Him. Because Christ lives in me, I too house the breath of God.

Hot Pink Trees

Three

Hot Pink Trees

PAINTING LIFE WITH COLOR AND PASSION

Three

My shirt hangs limply, clinging to the small of my back like cellophane on sticky candy. The temperature has dropped a bit with the sun, but the humidity hangs in there, pulling out any remaining curl in my hair. I can envision the smudges of mascara under my eyes.

My husband, four friends, and I have just arrived for a once-in-a-lifetime, dream vacation—ten days and nights on a catamaran in the Caribbean. It sounded impossibly exotic, back in February. Now our backs are cramped and our knees locked from hours of flying. I'm soggy as an overdressed salad, wondering, "Am I going to be this hot and this sticky for the entire ten days? Will I be seasick day *and* night?"

I actually had expectations of lying on our boat with a book. But my friends and husband nixed that idea from the beginning. They animated our pretrip discussions with their own expectations of speedboating, snorkeling, maybe even skin diving. I made my face eager, but inside my stomach churned.

I am not a water person. I like looking at the ocean, smelling the ocean, hearing the ocean. I don't even mind being on the ocean. But *in* the ocean? If God had wanted me in the water, He'd have given me webbed feet for confidence and naturally curly hair so I'd look better when I came out.

❧

My protests aside, after our first night in a very small bed in a very small cabin, I find myself being outfitted head to toe for my first "in the water" experience. I decide quickly there's nothing quite as odd looking as a person dressed for snorkeling.

First, you pull on swim fins and make your way awkwardly, heels first, down a ladder. Then you sit on the edge of the step and spit in your mask—that's right, spit, real spit. Rinsing that off in seawater, which isn't much different if you think about it, you stretch the mask like a girdle over your face, knowing you're making an imprint on your cheeks that will remain all the way into the evening.

Finally, you wedge the snorkel in your mouth, the same snorkel that has been in countless other mouths before yours. (But washed in bleach, Gus, the captain, assures.)

The skies are gray, rainy (where's all that sun in the brochure?). My face is suitably imprinted, my feet finned, and my mouth fixed in a permanent scream around the snorkel. I let myself, gingerly, down into the water.

But…it's warm! Maybe, just maybe, I can do this! (Courage is easier when your teeth aren't already chattering.) I try out my snorkel, put my face under the surface, kick a bit. There's a vast vista before me, a stillness and quietness in the water, yet a world thrilling with energy—and an enormous array of colorful fish.

᠁

Stillness in the midst of energy. Absolute quiet amid screams of color. Like these South Seas paradoxes, even the most serene still-life paintings are awash with the energy and passion of life and color. We've all seen a print of van Gogh's famous sunflowers—vibrant with bold yellows and oranges. He could have presented the *idea* of a sunflower in a simple sketch, but then it wouldn't shout, "Warm, summer, afternoon! Bliss, peace, delight!"

Color, you might say, is passion applied to painting. And passion is the very blood that makes a painting's image come alive. But passion—in life or in art—doesn't come without risk.

My artist neighbor, who paints flowers on her walls, explains that color takes courage. Often she prefers to use only shades she's accustomed to in her paintings. She'd rather repeat past successes than try something different. Why branch out with a new palette when the colors may take her someplace she doesn't want to go?

I know just how she feels. This vacation is an opportunity of a lifetime. A trip anyone would love to take. An invitation to passion. But it is still a risk for me. I didn't like the small plane from San Juan. I'm fearful about snorkeling and seasickness, and concerned about our captain and his wife. Will we all get along in such small quarters for ten whole days?

These things that keep me up at night are part and parcel of a wonderful adventure. But like my artist friend, I'm inclined to be timid, to do what is safest, familiar, and requires the least amount of hassle.

Isn't "safe" a big part of a still life? Isn't that one reason we call it "still"? Do "still" and "passion" mix at all? (Synonyms like "out of control" come to mind.) How is it possible to incorporate passion into life and retain the peace, calm, and quiet?

✢

Swimming, floating, on the surface of the water, my snorkel buddies and I head for the rocky reef. Raindrops gently patter on my head. I paddle along and am at once surrounded by a school of silvery slivers, then come almost nose to nose with a small barracuda floating nearly vertically in the water.

Without the sunlight, the fish are not as breathtakingly vivid as I've been promised, but that's all right. I'm not so breathtaking myself in this outfit.

Color is nonetheless essential in this world—for more than amusing tourists and giving birth to National Geographic photos. Some fish rely on their bright colors and interesting patterns to warn predators of their distasteful flesh. For others, color serves to attract a spouse.

55

On the other hand, some fish look so much like the coral or sea-weed in which they live, you have to look hard to see them. Flat fish like flounder and perch blend in with the sand and seaweed of the ocean floor. The lack of bright spots is their defense mechanism. For them, distinctive color could be deadly. They begin life swimming upright, like most fish. But as they grow, one of their eyes travels across their nose to the other side of their head. By the time that eye is situated right next to the other one, the fish is mature, swimming on its side and ready to be a bottom-dwelling creature, safe in its cam-ouflage.

For a long time my life has been safe, routine, predictable. Okay, okay, so I've been a bottom-dwelling creature. I've even used my chil-dren for camouflage now and then. (I check the mirror quickly to be sure my eyes are where they ought to be.) But these days, there are new things to consider, and the opportunities are beginning to collect around me like sea gulls around a fishing boat.

At one point while I was raising my kids, trying new things meant choosing another peanut butter. These days, when peanut butter is no longer a staple in my cupboard, I have a lot more choices and chal-lenges. But more often than not, they scare me.

How am I going to fill the time my empty nest will bring? Should I take a class even if it means I feel like an overaged dunce for a while? Am I ready to go along with Ron on his trips or comfortable enough to stay home, alone in our house with all the sliding glass doors? And of utmost and more immediate importance, should I color my hair or let the gray sparkle in the sunshine like fish scales?

With new opportunities come risk, fear, indecision, and challenge. On my best days, after my quiet time, with a cup of coffee, when I'm fully awake and in a good mood, I respond like a parrot fish—brightly colored, passionate, brave, and self-confident. When I'm awake in the middle of the night, though, I long for camouflage and anonymity.

I'm haunted by Marsha Sinetar's words: "Bland adjustment is the kiss of death to life."[1] In the long run, accepting the risk that passion invites is infinitely better than adapting to my surroundings, waiting for one eye to cross over and meet the other.

❧

My children have a book called *Uncle Bumble* that we read together when they were little. It's about a kind man who loses his home to urbanization. So he moves to the country, but before he can build his own house, he takes care of the animals' housing needs. In fact, he never gets around to building his home; but they, in their gratitude, do it for him one night when he's asleep.

I love this book not just because of the story. I love it because the trees are purple and the rabbits yellow and the deer pink. All the colors are topsy-turvy, far removed from what I see out my window, what I know is true.

When he was five, Matt's favorite crayon from the biggest Crayola box with the flip top was maize, actually a glorified yellow/gold. "What's your favorite color, Matt?" a primary-color adult would ask. "Maize," he'd say simply, to my delight and their puzzlement.

Children choose their colors with great creative abandon. Then all too often adults get involved and push for green trees and white rabbits. Creativity is stifled—and along with it, passion.

Passion and creativity are deeply linked by God Himself. He is the creator of passion, and He put within us an urge to passionately create. Unlike our Maker, we can't create something out of nothing. But we are creative any time we put together a combination that surprises, any time we stretch our minds around new thoughts, any time we do old things in a new and interesting way.

Passionate creativity is about coloring outside the lines, finding a fresh recipe for ground beef, wrapping birthday presents with a flair, buying bird-of-paradise blooms instead of roses for your mother. It's about risky vacations, challenging experiences, and new directions. It can be as simple as learning a new word or as complicated as painting a mural on a freeway viaduct.

❧

Reading the Old Testament, we couldn't possibly miss God's creative passion for detail, design, and beauty. He commanded the use of silver, gold, and bronze in the tabernacle structure and ordered priestly robes with a "skillfully woven waistband…made with gold, and with blue, purple and scarlet yarn, and with finely twisted linen." Aaron and his sons also wore a breastpiece with twelve different jewels set in gold filigree.[2]

Those must have been some glorious outfits. (And think about it: Any shoes they had on hand would match!)

I can imagine the pleasure God derived during His creation of the world and the pleasure He continues to give Himself as He maintains His artwork. He never stops creating, never stops being passionate and enthusiastic. And when we don't nurture our own creativity, when we stop approaching life with enthusiasm, we are not still within—but stifled. Not serene—but stagnant.

Creativity, however, does not have to be noisy or dramatic or boisterous or busy. It can be quiet, contemplative. Voltaire once wrote, "To listen, to observe, is in itself to be creative."

In fact, the earth is often silent when it is most creative. A chick growing inside of an egg. A daffodil bulb nudging toward earth's surface. Snow falling, alighting on the ground so silently we don't know it's snowing until the children look out of the window and squeal with joy.

❧

Could it really be snowing somewhere? Anywhere? It seems impossible, now that the sun has broken through here in the South Seas. I see blue skies like Easter eggs and beaches so bright with whiteness they sparkle like the stars in a hero's teeth. Everywhere I look colors are clear and brilliant; even the rocks look painted somehow.

Underwater, a ray of sun singles out the parrot fish and coral, spangling them with points of light that flash neon. According to the encyclopedia, our eyes can distinguish perhaps as many as ten million colors. Now I believe it's true. And that it's proof of creation. How could chance or evolution come up with such brilliant variety?

But I couldn't live this South Seas life for long. I couldn't give in to this vibrant color, this tropical sun, this bright life. It feels too intense, too close. And after a time I retreat to my tiny stateroom, to shade and shadow. I think about my children. I miss them. I want them to see what I'm seeing.

Does God dwell *here*? I know of course He does. I'm just not sure I can picture Him in a big straw hat or a tropical shirt with palm trees all over it. I've envisioned Him so regularly from my chair back home it's hard to imagine Him as comfortable in the net between the hulls on this catamaran, feeling the salt spray in His face.

At night, we lie outside on that net singing praises and thanksgiving to God, watching the shooting stars, feeling the breeze, snuggled together like sardines because it can be cool at night here. Our attention has moved from the sea to the sky, from color to black and white—another rendering of the passionate creativity of the Creator. And as myriad and fascinating as we know the creatures of the sea to be, the stars surpass them by far.

God's artistry radiates throughout the Caribbean, reminding me of the passionate lengths to which He's gone to express His love for us. But how fervent am I about expressing love and thanks to Him? Too often, I sit back in my deck chair, arms crossed, waiting for His blessings as if they are usual, expected, and rightfully mine.

No area of our lives is in greater need of conscious expression and expansion than our souls' passion for God. Writer Brennan Manning says that "passion is the essential energy of the soul." He's not talking about out-of-control emotion, but eagerness, zeal, enthusiasm. It's so easy to stay safe, to become lazy, to kick back and let our spiritual lives atrophy.

Certainly God doesn't want a forced response from us—nor does He want flamboyant emotion that's devoid of thought. John Piper says, "Emotion without truth produces empty frenzy and cultivates shallow people who refuse the discipline of rigorous thought. But true worship comes from people who are deeply emotional and who love deep and sound doctrine. Strong affections for God rooted in truth are the bone and marrow of biblical worship."[3]

We worship God when we respond to His gifts—creation, salvation, relationship, Christ Himself—with some of the emotion He employed in giving them to us. He knows we're unique individuals with our own feelings, our own inhibitions, our own ways of expressing passion. He also longs to be loved and noticed by His supreme creation—us.

Passion is not something we put on or nonchalantly dismiss as we walk out of church. It is a rich, burning intensity to know God better and at a deeper level than before. It's a willingness to stand open armed in front of the force of His personality, ready to receive whatever He wants to breathe into us. It's a fervor to become more than we are.

If we feel passionately about Christ, it will show in our obedience. Jesus says repeatedly, "If you love Me, obey Me." Looking for the emotion without the responsibility doesn't work. "Often we mistakenly pursue the deeper life rather than obedience," says Calvin Miller. "Most people live powerlessly today. They prefer to live in indulgence.... They choose ease and complain that they find no deep satisfaction in Christ. Self-will always hungers for the fruits of obedience without the effort of it."[4]

Passionate obedience is work. It has very little to do with whether we pray with our eyes open or closed, or whether we wave our arms in praise during the singing. It has everything to do with a relationship with the living God—a relationship established by time and faithfulness. Just as we expect a close friend or spouse to be there day after day, so God wants to see our faces and our hearts on a frequent basis.

True spiritual passion is a daily commitment to fully experience God. And when we get in the habit of that truth-filled enthusiasm, it will show in our faith and in our lives.

It's our last night here. A night we've set aside for dinner on the beach of a beautiful island. We shower, as best we can. Sea soap in our hair and over our swimsuited bodies; a quick dip in the bay to rinse off; an even quicker spray with the fresh water on the boat to finish the job. Not quite my idea of luxury, but I make do. We dress up a little—skirts, slacks, shoes for a change. I wear my lovely straw hat—no hair dryer or curling iron at my disposal, so I make do there as well.

We clamber aboard the dinghy and motor the short distance to the white beach. Just as we're nearly grounded, we jump out and wade onto the sand, shoes dangling from our fingers.

Dinner is memorable. We know we're in trouble when one person seats us, another brings water, another brings us soft drinks from the bar, another takes our order, and still another asks how we're doing. The food is good enough, the view of the sunset and the water unparalleled, the company perfect. The check...astronomical. Ah, well. It's our last night here.

We pay it, trembling, and walk on the beach. All of us sit in a hammock, swinging hard. "Be careful," I admonish, preparing to be dumped in the sand if it breaks. "Take a risk," my friend chides me. He's right. I brace myself. It doesn't break.

We whistle our call to Gus and he brings the dinghy. Shoes off, we make a dash for it, and somehow this trip our timing's awry. The dinghy goes over, dumps poor Gus in the surf, and reduces the men to waterlogged lackeys as they right it for the women. I enjoy being a girl.

❧

I've never wanted to be a sedentary woman, but somehow it happened—in between the courageous abandon of youth and the set-in-my-ways habits of middle age. Thankfully, and fearfully, I'm now watching God disturb those fixed habits and bring a little passion my way. More hunger for robust life. Not always loud, blow-out life; sometimes nearly invisible activity, like swinging in a hammock and watching the clouds. But now and then it requires that I throw off my old familiar clothes and don some costumes I never even imagined would look good on me. Like a snorkel and swim fins.

Passion asks us to push away the comfortable and slip off the boat into the water.

But ultimately, passion is a gift we give back to life and to ourselves. It doesn't rob us of our still lives; it makes them richer, deeper, more real. It enables us to say we are living life fully, fervently, the way God intended. Genuine passion declares that God is good and because He is good, life is good and it's worth pouring ourselves into. It's worth taking risks and being creative if we can bring more beauty and meaning to each other and the world.

Thank goodness we were not meant to be bottom-dwellers, merely adapting to our surroundings. Our destiny is to be a van Gogh sunflower or the brightest fish in the sea—like a stoplight parrot fish, all decked out in turquoise and purple and yellow. So shout for joy! Swim for your life! Clap your hands when no one can hear. "Shout for joy, O heavens; rejoice, O earth; burst into song."[5]

For tomorrow the trees may be pink and all the sky turn the color of maize.

A Long Night's Dance

Four

A Long Night's Dance

EMBRACING LIGHT AND SHADOW

Underneath Mom's new Nancy Reagan wig was a bald head I hadn't yet seen. Her smart clothes had been left behind. Shuffling down the airport corridor with my sister, she looked like someone else's elderly mother—T-shirt and sweater, sweatpants, sneakers, and sport socks—slower in step and with a dimness that belied her natural enthusiasm. I couldn't fling my arms around her neck and start my customary non-stop chatter; nor could I sneak up behind her and surprise her as I might have done in the past. For the first time in my life she was fragile, porcelain, opalescent.

Waving to give plenty of warning, I walked toward her, willing the moistness out of my eyes. "Hi, you sweet thing," I nuzzled in her neck. My sister and I exchanged knowing looks, the kind mothers share over their children's heads.

And so began our last four months together, months of elation and frustration, peace and confusion, light and shadow.

෨

The pears on the cover of this book are awash in light. We don't know what's causing the light, but anyone can see where it's coming from. The pears appear to turn their "faces" to it, and the light coats the edges of the stems and the fruit delicately, almost like the kiss you gently draw along the cheek of a sleeping child.

But imagine the pears without that light. If we could see them at all, they'd appear artificial, without a trace of juicy flesh.

Without the effects of light a work of art is flat and lifeless. Artists spend nearly as much time testing and adjusting the way the light falls on their subjects as they spend portraying the subjects themselves. Where is the light coming from? they ask. How does it affect my subjects?

Shadows get equal attention. They're not merely accidental spaces of darkness. It's the shadows that bring out the three-dimensional character of the painting. They create the depth. A painted pear with no shading becomes merely a shape, a symbol.

The same principles are true in an authentic or "still" life. A life of depth, a life lived fully, includes both light and shadow, joy and pain. Henri Nouwen says, "Joy and sadness are as close to each other as the splendid colored leaves of a New England fall to the soberness of the barren trees.... Joy and sadness are born at the same time, both arising from such deep places in your heart that you can't find words to capture your complex emotions."[1]

Reflecting on those last four months with my mother, I can see both sides. Even though at times I felt engulfed in darkness, the interplay of light and shadow made the time rich and the memories wondrous.

❧

I went out for my walk today and found my car had been broken into. For two hours I dealt with the police and the insurance company. The loss of property was minimal; the loss of time enormous. It's not a heavy shadow, but it is one nonetheless.

We schedule our days, make our goals, buy the planning notebooks. We assume that next month, on Tuesday, we'll be free for lunch with our best friend. Then our children get strep throat; our cars are broken into; our husbands lose their jobs. Our mothers get cancer.

Who wants pain and stress, beneficial as they may be? Don't all dark times awaken our natural instincts for self-preservation and make us want to run? The hope of God using our troubles for good isn't enough to make us welcome them.

My first response to trials is to lessen the pain and ignore the lesson. The majority of my prayers focus on besieging God to remove some pressure from my life—the pressure of fear, or hard work, or uncertainty, or functioning outside my comfort zone.

Yet even as I write this, I cringe at the thought that the pursuit of ease is a shallow one indeed. A one-dimensional life, with no stress, no challenge (or maybe the denial of the dark), seems so wasteful, so meaningless.

Don't we all have a pocket inside us that we long to fill with a brave and successful encounter with hardship? Don't we secretly want to be numbered with the women who endure, the women who fight and conquer the odds?

Most likely. But that desire flies in the face of what we *feel* in the middle of our blackest hours.

~

Beginning artists make the mistake (at least I did) of assuming shadows are simply shades of black and gray. Actually, shadows have color because they're caused by the reflection of light shining on something. The shadow of a plum has purple in it. The shadow of a green leaf, green. The shadow of a golden pear, gold.

In the same way, circumstances in our lives cast shadows with their own colors. They come from our falleness, from sin and mistakes, from our choices to walk in dark places. Who can we blame when our checks bounce?

Other times, shadows come because we *live* in a fallen world. Sickness, persecution. My mother's cancer. God doesn't necessarily spare his children. Think of the apostle Paul and all his hardships—shipwrecks, rejection, prison, beatings, even what he called his "thorn in the flesh."

Often shadows are the result of natural blessings. My friend who lives in the woods regularly exclaims over the goodness of her life— her sensitive husband, her five exemplary kids, her beautiful home with the five bedrooms and bathrooms *and* the river rock fireplace she'd always dreamed of.

But hang around her house long enough, and you can spot the natural shadows that God's blessings have cast. "All I do is shuttle my kids back and forth from practice to games to rehearsals…. Have you ever tried to keep up with cleaning five bathrooms?" When she first moved into that house, I could hear her voice echo over the telephone in the empty rooms. Now there's no echo, just stuff to dust and keep clean.

So is God present in some of our shadows and absent in others? Hardly. Every dark place we enter has God's fingerprints in grand relief all over it. Even the consequences of our own sin are no surprise to God. He's involved. We just have to look a bit to see His color.

One friend of mine finds it in the shadow of a past she'd like to forget. God already has, and He's using it in her life as a springboard of compassion for others. Another friend finds His color in the eyes of her out-of-wedlock granddaughter. Her unexpected conception has nevertheless produced a life created in the image of God, and she's loved just for that (and a whole lot of other reasons).

No darkness is truly complete because nothing can separate us from the love of God in Christ Jesus.[2] Some light, some color, will always be present.

ॐ

Mom came to my home in California for seven weeks in the summer of 1990 to give my sisters a respite from her care, and to help me understand what they and she were going through. It was an eye-opener. Her non-Hodgkins lymphoma had recently spread undetected to her brain. There it pushed aside short-term memory and the ability to perform certain habitual tasks we take for granted.

Numerous little oddities defined each day. Mom set the table with three forks at this place, two knives and a spoon at that one. She poured orange juice into the coffee thermos and wrapped drippy watermelon in paper towels to store in the refrigerator.

Getting her dressed became a group activity.

Everything we did that summer took longer than I thought it would. Mom gave simple tasks the same weight as weekend forays to the mountains. I wrestled with my impatience, astonished and embarrassed that this woman, this mother, could elicit any other emotion from me than affection. At those moments, her neurologist's reprimand came most painfully to mind. "Remember, she's doing the best she can."

I wondered about the darkness that was taking over my mother's clever mind. Was she aware of the paths she was walking now? Did she sense the darkness? Did she notice the light going out of her eyes when she looked in the mirror?

When my mother's cancer had moved from the positive ("The doctor says it's treatable!") to the not so positive ("She's got another lump"), I moved God from the early morning quiet-time box to moment-by-moment conversation (which I'm quite sure is where He'd like to be all the time).

I remember walking the track behind our house (it was a chilly day, unfriendly in so many ways) saying, "Oh God, oh God, oh God, oh God." My husband, kind as he is, couldn't have tolerated my yammering. "Heal her, heal her," I repeated over and over. I didn't know what to say or how to beg God with an entreaty powerful enough to sway what I feared was His plan.

My friend Connie knows what that's like. She is blessed with an unusual talent for music and lyrics. For years she's written praise music with her husband and used their platform as worship leaders to sing the good news of Christ. Her lyrics are poetry, not chronology or story, and her performances are offerings to the God who is there.

Last year Connie was diagnosed with multiple sclerosis. She hit the brick wall of disbelief and unreality, and staggered under the ponderous weight of a future that's not so unknown anymore. She appealed for prayer, understanding, and support. She solicited meals, rides, and assistance. She waited to disintegrate into an ill, unused shadow of herself.

"It's dark everywhere I turn," I can hear her say. "And the trouble is, I can't flick on the light. Aren't shadows supposed to be temporary? When the sun comes up, the shadows slide away. But what if you're in a situation where you know the sun won't come up in quite the same way again?"

I understand her question. It echoes similar ones I asked as I watched my mother sink into darkness. It's a question women ask who are raising their children alone, whose homes are war zones, or who are working at two jobs just to stay afloat. Of what importance is the pursuit of a still life when survival is first on our minds?

Paul's survival was often in question too. In 2 Corinthians 4 he writes, "We are hard pressed on every side, but not crushed; perplexed, but not in despair; persecuted, but not abandoned; struck down, but not destroyed.... Though outwardly we are wasting away, yet inwardly we are being renewed day by day. For our light and momentary troubles are achieving for us an eternal glory that far outweighs them all."[3]

I look through Paul's list of "shadows" and skip over to chapter 6, where he adds "hardships and distresses;...beatings, imprisonments and riots;...hard work, sleepless nights and hunger" to his list of "light and momentary troubles."

What was it about Paul that made his troubles "light and momentary"? If he can describe his persecution in such terms, can Connie do the same? Can we?

I call up a quote from Victor Frankl that has a glimmer of an answer. He said, "Despair is suffering without meaning."

We despair when our adversity seems to have no purpose. I love Paul's conclusions in Romans 5: "We also rejoice in our sufferings, because we know that suffering produces perseverance; perseverance, character; and character, hope. And hope does not disappoint us."[4]

"Suffering must not be avoided, but embraced," says Eugene Peterson. "Brokenness does not diminish a life of faith but deepens it."[5]

Though we talk of avoiding the difficult times, they round out who we are. They shape and display our character; they give weight to our personality. "Perseverance produces character…"

When we run away, we don't escape the shadows; we keep them from giving richness and power to our lives.

So what does it mean to embrace suffering, to "persevere" in hardship?

Alan Nelson writes, "When we go through difficult issues without developing an awareness of our inadequacies and God's love for us, we become broken in the wrong places."[6] God urges us to lean into the shadows, to accept and use our pain, and learn the lessons He has for us. To resist, to stiffen, might be to snap.

During my mother's illness and dying, I knew deep within me it was important to let myself feel the pain fully. As much as I didn't want *any* part of it, I knew I needed *every* part of it. Only then would I be able to walk through the whole experience and come out on the other side having found a purpose in the suffering. How interesting it is that God uses one woman's crucible to purify another.

When we embrace difficulties, we learn about ourselves—our weaknesses, blind spots, inadequacies—and we let ourselves be broken in the *right* places. That kind of brokenness leads to the character Paul talks about. Then the shadows have meaning. It helps to think that all we're going through won't be wasted. Suffering gives us energy when we're able to say, "How I handle this is important."

Connie resigned her church music position but is still singing songs that lift her questions and hurt out of her gut and up to the Lord. "Interestingly enough," Connie says, "I'm living and walking through the lyrics of songs the Lord has given me over the last twenty years. I wrote them—but now I am experiencing them."

Shaped by her experience, her songs are tributes to what God is letting her see. She's also writing articles and consoling other MS sufferers who, no doubt, have never met a songbird like Connie.

Connie chose to accept her shadows and is now using what is good in them. She's lost her hold on the familiar handles of life, but her grip is stronger in His hand.

It wasn't easy. I doubt she'd recommend it. But I know she believes this: Darkness holds surprising treasures.

❧

Mom went back to Denver in September. I think I knew she would die soon. I wish, I wish we could have talked about death. For years we had talked about everything else. We had shared laughter so unrelenting we would have to leave the room to breathe. We shared confidences, prayers, hopes, jokes, books, recipes, and politics. We could have talked about death as well, but now, watching her puzzled look about everyday trivia, I knew it would be too much for her.

I wanted to reassure her that everything would be okay. That dying is part of everything we are. That the God we both confessed was no dream but a real Being who was orchestrating her last months and waiting eagerly for her arrival.

As I wrestled with my own emotions and attempted to manifest some shred of strength and stillness in that "summer of my mother," Mom just sat there, quietly letting it all happen around her. "Honey," she finally reassured me one warm morning, "being around you is like slipping on a comfortable old shoe."

Mom spent her last two weeks in my sister Katharine's home, with almost constant attendance from us and our aunt, who helped with the decisions, daily struggles, and administration that are a part of dying. Hospice was there to answer our questions, stepping in when we needed reassurance or comfort. The last few nights we bunked in her room, curled in chairs or sleeping bags.

She died in our sleep.

My psalm that morning was Psalm 30, which closes with these words: "You turned my wailing into dancing; you removed my sackcloth and clothed me with joy, that my heart may sing to you and not be silent. O LORD my God, I will give you thanks forever."[7]

It was odd to read those verses (and a previous one, "Will the dust praise you? Will it proclaim your faithfulness?") in the context of such a great loss.

Did Paul *really* say, "Rejoice in the Lord always!"?

He shouts this by letter to the Philippians while a prisoner. "I will say it again: Rejoice!" In the middle of dark, dark times he delivered his happiest words, his most joyful message. "Do not be anxious about anything, but in everything, by prayer and petition, with thanksgiving, present your requests to God. And the peace of God, which transcends all understanding, will guard your hearts and your minds in Christ Jesus."[8]

My Bible opens without prompting to those verses, I've been there so many times. I quote them when my children have fevers, when I need to say something difficult to a friend, when I wake up overwhelmed with a messy house and a full schedule. When my mother was dying. They resonate with purpose and meaning. They take every situation and give it a framework that holds the parts together. They promise that in every circumstance, every shadow, I *can* have hope, light, and joy.

When we fix our eyes on the Light, and on the Word, we begin to see through God's eyes. And that changes our perspective, our fear, our future. Even our circumstances are affected, if only by the change in our attitudes.

God's light is all around us and even more astonishingly within us as well. I'm struck with the wonder that God lives inside me! Not in a pantheistic way, as in "God is in everything," but in the miraculous way that the immutable, indescribable God has shrunk His majesty to fit inside my humanity. My femaleness. He didn't have to be so available. He didn't have to live in me.

Paul writes, "For God, who said, 'Let light shine out of darkness,' made His light shine in our hearts to give us the light of the knowledge of the glory of God in the face of Christ."[9] When we belong to Christ, the Light of the World, He dwells in us like a lamp that will never go out. Like a painted pear with a night-light tucked in its core, breaking all the rules...

❧

The morning my mom died we three sisters and our aunt took what we later called The Walk. Marching like Rockettes down the middle of the street, we dared any motorist to break us up, exulting in the early morning crispness, relieved for ourselves and Mom that the ordeal was over. We sang, we laughed, we cried, we walked in silence, breathing deeply, arms locked all the way.

The day of her funeral was beautiful. Colorado in November, and, strangely enough, the air still warm, the grass still green. Clouds like beaten egg whites scudded across the sky; geese wandered among the gravestones at the cemetery. The sanctuary filled with friends who loved her, who laughed along with us at remembrances of funny things that had happened to her or at witticisms she had offered. Light and shadow. It was a grand send-off.

Honestly, for much of my life I worried about how I'd react to the death of my mother, my friend. I was confident of her eternal life but desperately uncomfortable with how I'd handle my loss. But my mother did die and I got through it. Even though God didn't do all I wanted Him to do, He did more than I could ask or think. He fleshed out in my experience all that He promised in His Word He'd be. And in doing so, He convinced me that He would be true to His Word in the future as well.

"This intimate experience in which every bit of life is touched by a bit of death can point us beyond the limits of our existence," says Henri Nouwen. "It can do so by making us look forward in expectation to the day when our hearts will be filled with perfect joy, a joy that no one shall take away from us."[10]

When we look at our shadows as created by, or allowed by, the light of God, they become precious to us. They're part of a plan, they have a reason. Not only are they necessary to the moment, but they also have a transforming quality in our lives. We are not flat, two-dimensional people. In Christ, we have depth, hope, and peace.

Whatever is going on in our homes, in our minds, in our hearts we can gather from the shadows without succumbing to them! Even as we wait in those shadows, we are not alone. "He who dwells in the shelter of the Most High will rest in the shadow of the Almighty."[11]

I'm dwelling. I'm resting. I'm waiting.

Freckled Apples

Five

Freckled Apples

CELEBRATING THE ORDINARY

It's October. My son with the artist's soul has sent me a box full of fall leaves from Chicago for my birthday. I suspect it's leaves when I pick up the box and feel nothing. He's sent me leaves before. He knows San Diego at this time of year is bereft of color and that my heart hankers for the brisk, brilliant autumns of my Colorado childhood.

(Now and then our sweet gum trees—the only trees in our yard which drop their leaves in the winter—let loose some Colorado scarlet if they try hard enough. I check every day to see.)

My sisters Katharine and Annie are with me as I pull out the brilliant, fragile leaves, one after another. We are struck by how these ordinary bits of creation become extraordinary when we pull them from a box rather than off the ground.

∾

Sometimes the commonplace is comforting, wonderful. Crinkly, scarlet fall leaves, a profusion of fresh oranges spilling out of a big blue bowl, a family dinner with everyone talking at once.

But more often, that big blue bowl is just another bowl I see every morning, the family dinners with everyone in attendance are too hard to pull off, and the covering of fall leaves signals hours of raking ahead.

Life isn't always made up of brilliant colors, bright light, and deep shadows—sometimes it's so monochromatic, so much the same, so ordinary, we can't stand it anymore.

Annie just called. Her five-year-old son is whining about the rainy weather. Both of them have cabin fever. Every day Annie picks up Legos and art projects, balances carpools and trips to the grocery store, walks and brushes their new puppy who's already bigger than they expected him to be full grown. To Annie, who has lots of deciduous trees, fall leaves just mean another task on her to-do list.

How can she transform the mundane aspects of being a wife and mother into something more meaningful? How can any busy woman?

I think most of us wonder at times. Our lives take place in ordinary settings amid ordinary activities. It's natural to be weary of the "daily," or to try to exchange it for something more exciting.

For some reason, what's ordinary and mundane to me seems extraordinary to my sisters. And vice versa. Too bad we can't wrap our lives up in a box and send them to each other. Maybe they'd look different to us then.

In a way, that's what a still-life artist does—takes the ordinary things around her and repackages them. In fact, one of the greatest hallmarks of a still-life painting is the use—even the glorification—of ordinary objects. Forks, knives, and coffee mugs strewn about on the table—there's almost always a table. Books stacked, randomly it seems, among musical instruments, or breakfast. Garden-variety flowers. Fruit—blemished or not, whole or partly eaten. Things that move in and out of everyday life are brought forward and celebrated.

In art and in life, an authentic still life is one that embraces, even celebrates, the ordinary. But, understandably, it's harder for a woman to develop an affection for the ordinary when she can't pick and choose her "subjects." What if all she sees around her are unmade beds, piles of ironing, and sacks of groceries that need to be put away?

If we can't change the ordinary subjects in our lives, then perhaps, like artists, we can change the way we view them.

❧

All art depends upon the artist's power of observation, but still-life artists rely on their vision in a unique way. We might attribute the beauty of a painting of the Alps to the fantastic natural scenery, or a portrait's beauty to the glamour of the subject. But who can explain how a loaf of bread becomes art, aside from the artist's creative vision?

Andy Warhol was famous for his still-life paintings of everyday objects. He effectively immortalized a Coke bottle by turning it into a work of art and hanging it on a wall. It was just an ordinary bottle, but because he saw it with an artist's eye, he changed the way we saw it as well.

Jesus Himself saw the ordinary, not just with an artist's eye, but also with a storyteller's eye for metaphor. "To make his truth both memorable and usable," Calvin Miller points out, "[Jesus] worked with what was close at hand: wildflowers, fig trees, mustard seeds, lamps, baskets, shepherds, sheep, weeds and wheat."[1]

It's tempting to attribute a special aura to the simple things Jesus chose. Or to note that Andy Warhol was an artistic genius. We wonder if it takes a certain talent, or divinity, to touch up the ordinary activities—to add depth and highlights to the elements of life until we can see them as art, as compelling, as part of life's great meaning.

But, surely, recognizing the glory of the ordinary is possible even for the most "ordinary" among us. Observation is an intentional decision, and so the better question is probably, are we really looking? Have we really *seen* what we saw?

Ruth Senter says in *Secrets from Ordinary Places*, "If I would 'look well…to this day,' I must learn the power of observation. How does the wind feel in my face as I take my morning walk along Klein Creek? How high is the water under the bridge? What stage are the crab-apple blossoms in? How did my neighbor look today when I passed her on the path?"[2]

I can imagine that Brother Lawrence asked similar questions. He lived and worked several hundred years ago in a monastery and saw the unique worth in every thing and every action.[3] Raking leaves, he'd thank God for their profusion. Working in the kitchen was a joy because he saw it as an act of service to God.

I think of *my* kitchen. Is it possible, for instance, to see an apple in such a way that it takes on new significance? I try it. Instead of merely rinsing one quickly and dropping it in Molly's lunch bag, I take time to notice the deep, deep red of its skin and the smooth freckles that pepper the top. I think it goes pretty well.

Yesterday on my walk, I took the path that's bordered by Brazilian pepper trees. Often when I walk underneath them, I'm conscious of a hum, as if the trees are letting me know just how hard they're working. The sound comes from bees in such abundance throughout the branches that they look like little bits of fruit hanging, hovering, there.

Creation is glorious! Even though I see the same trees and leaves and birds day after day, I have no trouble finding God on my walks in the morning, or at night under the stars. I'm alert to Him in nature and even to what He might want to teach me. "We speak words; God speaks things," Virginia Stem Owens says. "He opens what we suppose to be his metaphorical mouth, and out tumble trees, viruses, moons."[4]

Even so, the rest of my life I'm up to my eyelids in man-made stuff—in newspapers and taxes and unironed shirts. It's much more of a challenge to see and celebrate *these* everyday things.

My dad was good at this. When Matt was little, Dad lifted him high in the kitchen so he could see in the top shelves of the cabinets; held him before the open freezer door so he could feel the cold air on his face; taught him how to use a light switch. He showed him how to work the elevator in his twelve-story apartment building, how the trash went down the chute and where it ended up. He took him out on the balcony to look with binoculars over all the city.

He taught Matt to send his mother leaves in the mail.

Although Molly's style is a little less poetic and a little more practical, in her own way she also has learned to lay claim to the ordinary.

When Ron and I married twenty-seven years ago, his mother gave us a set of bowls she'd bought at her corner gas station with a fill-up. There was nothing special about them, except that we didn't have much in our kitchen and they fulfilled a need. Over the years most of them broke, but two have tenaciously held on to this life, like the final leaves of fall.

Last year at garage-sale time, I stacked those ugly bowls in a box of twenty-five-cent "treasures," along with countless mugs and odd pieces of everyday dishware. Next thing I knew, they were back in the cupboard.

"Molly!" I yelled up the stairs. "Why did you take these crummy bowls out of the box?"

"Because I love them!" she yelled back.

⁓

I crawled out of bed this morning in a gray, surly frame of mind. Not even my coffee or my hot shower was enough to wake me fully, and there was no time for a walk with Homer. I have fifteen errands to do, several letters to answer, phone calls to make, and my car needs an oil change and the air conditioning fixed. My eyes fall on the dishwasher that needs unloading. It's an ordinary day, and the Caribbean's a distant memory. I'd pull my hair out, but I don't have any to spare.

What do we women do with days like today? We try to change the outside, to see what's around us in a different way. We try to paint our lives with passion, but sometimes the ordinary just takes over.

As I put away the clean glasses, I wonder if it's the circumstances or my response to them that's the problem. Maybe if I deal with my attitude, these everyday irritations won't wield such power in my life.

I've heard it said that even if we make up our minds to change our behavior, our bodies must follow through with a change as well, or we have a less-than-likely chance of success. So I determine to change the way my day is going and decide to smile at everyone I pass on my fifteen errands. On the way out of the grocery store, I nod and smile at a middle-aged man. He asks me for a date. Oh, brother.

That experience aside, I notice a difference in my day. The end is better than the beginning. Just that decision—to view it all in a different light and show it by a smile—changes my attitude and my behavior.

❧

Calvin Miller calls us to go a step farther, to transform the ordinary things around us by seeing them through spiritual eyes, by "Christifying" them. "Christifying is consciously viewing the people and circumstances in our lives with the eyes of Christ. Ordinary events become cosmic when seen this way. Ordinary people explode with meaning as we see their potential salvation and service to the Holy Christ. In Christifying, the whole world will speak to us and shout to us of the reality of God. Francis Thompson said he could not even pick a flower without causing an inner trembling in the distant stars."[5]

We Christify, and "sanctify," ordinary things by using them as they were intended to be used, or by taking time to register their beauty—ladles by serving the soup with them, apples by noticing their freckles on top. We Christify ordinary activities—ironing, cooking, our jobs—by seeing them as acts of service, by doing them joyfully, by praying during them.

We Christify ordinary people (is any person *really* ordinary?) by acknowledging their divine image and forgiving their humanity. Here we arrive at the central question: In the long run, does it matter so much how we see ordinary *objects,* if we can't learn to see ordinary *people* with God's vision?

My sister Katharine sees people that way. Every beggar in the street receives something from her—money or a kind smile or a hand up to their feet—for she sees them with a vision for their potential, their value. No one is ordinary in her eyes. She looks at strangers, and at Annie and me, as so important to the scheme of things.

From her example, I now look at the faces of the people I pass on the street or in the airport. Some move me to prayer, and I'm grateful

I can count on God to know their needs. I'm learning to Christify others by praying God's mercy and blessing down on their heads.

This evening I walk through my house, remembering the times I've knelt by the beds of my children in the middle of the night when they were sick or troubled. How long has it been since I've Christified the space they live in by praying over it? Rolling my husband's socks into little packets, I thank God his feet don't stray, that he's exercising more regularly, that he has enough socks. (I think of a woman who prays for her husband's arms as she irons his shirts.)

Christifying our families means actually imagining them in God's presence; means withholding nothing of them from Him (as if we could); means relaxing in the truth that all of His nature will watch over them.

Our one act of faith releases us all.

⁓

Christifying is also a way to remind ourselves not to take the ordinary for granted, but to be pleased and content with who and what we have. The ordinary is fragile and much more precious than we realize.

When Matt came home for a break from school, bringing five

college friends with him, I was thrilled to be cooking—the daily task I used to resent the most. It had been a long time since I'd prepared three meals a day for Matt, much less a whole team of friends. Suddenly the ordinary was transformed—and in the middle of the work I felt an inner peace.

Coming to terms with the ordinary helps us create a tranquil soul. And yet, it is a tranquil soul we need in order to transform the way we see our lives! The process is really a cycle.

When all is said and done, a still life doesn't merely take place in the middle of ordinary surroundings. In a subtle way it changes those surroundings, and those people, even those gas station bowls, into something set apart, sacred, shining with a light we've not seen before.

❧

Weeks later, I look out my window and...they've done it! My sweet gum trees have hit the big-time color for a change! I bet that every person driving up our street nearly runs over the curb when they see them. I immediately go outside and gather up a handful of leaves to send to Matt.

It's snowing where he is now.

Elephant Studies

Elephant Studies

COMPOSING THE BIG PICTURE

Today is the Monday before Thanksgiving. I stand at the sink polishing silver, picturing the table when it's full of pomp and circumstance. It's a strangely satisfying experience—rubbing polish into the filigree on my serving dishes, smoothing it into the roundness of my tea and coffee service. Not at all like shining the chrome in the bathroom.

In the afternoon I walk the aisles at the store, basket to basket with enough people to fill a stadium. Along with the overabundance of starch and sweets the holidays require, I pile in firm, crisp apples, perfectly round oranges and grapefruit, long, slender bananas, and green and red peppers so true to color we should plan Christmas around them.

What is it about fruits and vegetables that is so pleasing to the human eye?

I have a conversation about this with my artist neighbor who paints wispy grasses on her living room walls. We talk about the subjects we're most attracted to in art. I'm a fruit person. She's a flower child.

She challenges me to consider the whole of a painting. What transforms those objects we love from a collection to an arrangement, from a stack of objects to a beautiful statement? She explains the importance of composition in creating a beautiful still life. In part, it's knowing how to bring all the elements together, she says. The flowers—or fruits—must be understood in relationship to the other objects. In composition, *everything* is connected in one way or another.

The same is true in our lives. My ancient dictionary defines composition as "the art or practice of so combining the parts of a work of art as to produce a harmonious whole." This is the goal of my life—and even of my Thanksgiving dinner.

We have an innate longing for harmony that comes from God. Everything He made has a place, a purpose and a reason for being where and like it is. We see it in the rising and setting of the sun, in the perfect peas lined up inside their pods, in our own longing for some controlled routine, for some sense of order in our lives.

But wanting and achieving are two different things. How easy for the artist to focus on the vase at the expense of the flowers, for me to overcook the stuffing while I peel the potatoes—for all of us to lose the vision of the whole and get sucked into juggling tiny pieces of our existence.

In 1783, artist Sir Joshua Reynolds commented on the difficulty of good composition. "Every [one] that can paint at all can execute individual parts; but to keep those parts in due subordination as relative to a whole, requires a comprehensive view of the art, that more strongly implies genius, than perhaps any other quality."[1]

How did this man know it would be so hard to be a woman over two hundred years later?

Anne Lindbergh said, with some wistfulness, "The problem is not merely one of *Woman and Career, Woman and the Home, Woman and Independence.* It is more basically: how to remain whole in the midst of the distractions of life; how to remain balanced, no matter what centrifugal forces tend to pull one off center."[2]

&

So how do all the elements of a still life work together to form the harmonious whole that God seems to imply is possible?

I thought I had some answers when I started this book. "Find simplicity. Clean your house!" I was prepared to admonish. But cleaning wasn't the answer. I had to look to discover what simplicity really was.

And soon after, I shouted to myself, "Get some space! Take time away!" But as I wrote, I had to ask, "For what? To where?"

In fact, I was surprised to discover that each facet of a still life was complete only when it ended in a deeper spiritual understanding.

For many years I've worked on the assumption that some day I'd be so in control of the different elements of my life that I'd achieve, once and for all, that harmonious whole. But for all my efforts, I've concluded that control is beyond my power.

Does this mean the goal setting I did year after year was a waste? I don't think so—goals are important and useful—but maybe I didn't go far enough. I planned all the elements of my composition but didn't relate them to the whole. I chose my fruits but laid them out in a row on the table instead of piling them together in a center-piece.

It takes more than a handful of carefully reasoned parts to end up with a well-composed life. Up to now, we've focused in tightly on simplicity, passion, light and shadow, white space, ordinary objects. But while each of these alone has a lot to offer, we need a wider, longer view of our lives to see the big picture.

Eventually an artist (and a woman) senses when it's time to pull back and check the overall composition. Am I seeing things from the right perspective? What is my focal point to be? Is my center drawn strongly enough to harmonize all that revolves around it? What message is my life sending?

I asked myself that question about the art on the cover of this book when I first saw it—what is the artist trying to communicate here? I sensed peace, quiet, tranquillity. The total composition—not the pears themselves, not the light, or the colors—sends this message.

Really, it's this big picture, the whole composition of our lives, that *has* to make sense. Viewed bit by bit, sometimes the pieces don't look as if they'll fit. We're like the three blind men who each examined a different part of an elephant. One considered the trunk and said, "An elephant is like a snake." One felt a leg and said, "An elephant is like a tree." The third studied the tail and said, "No, an elephant is like a rope." None of them understood the whole elephant.

Our goal too is to see and bring harmony to the whole of our lives —not just the work part, the children part, or the busy day-to-day stuff. Certainly that's where much of our *time* goes. But the composition of a still life also includes aspects such as passion and solitude. Combined, all these parts work together and resonate from our lives to say to the world, "peace, joy, stillness."

❧

That's a trick for Thanksgiving too—getting everything (and everyone!) to work together. The day before, Ron helps me add a leaf to the dining table. I find my grandmother's white tablecloth, the only one that fits the stretched-out size, and set out all those wedding presents we use only once or twice a year. Molly adds the napkins (nice big paper ones I won't have to wash) and the silverware and a big stack of plates.

In the afternoon I chop celery and onions for the stuffing, pick up my twenty-three-pound turkey, and then rush to the newest warehouse grocery. I've just heard that their pies (pecan, apple, and pumpkin) are a full twelve inches in diameter. For the first time in years, I buy all the pies instead of baking them. They're the most beautiful things I've ever seen.

Early Thanksgiving morning I wake up to a house warm and fragrant with the baking bird (this year I cooked the turkey overnight on the advice of a friend who says the moist meat will fall off the bones). With coffee in hand, I recheck the dining table, mentally calculating what and who will go where. Then I get out the sack of potatoes I need to peel.

Working on these potatoes reminds me of my dad. Turkey dinners with all the trimmings, especially mashed potatoes and gravy, were his favorite meal. So much so, in anticipation he didn't eat anything else all day.

In my parents' home, we dressed up for Thanksgiving dinner. Daddy would wear a coat and tie, but that formality did not restrain his humor. Every holiday he'd delight us three sisters and our cousins with his magic tricks—swallowing a dinner knife right before our very eyes and retrieving quarters from our ears. As we grew older, he entertained us with his impersonations of Jack Benny, arms crossed, looking off in the distance with disdain.

When I was little, sometimes after dinner he'd dance with me to the Mills Brothers—I in my stocking feet standing on his shoes. He'd hum in my ear, off-tune but involved, and bend his daddy-sized frame to rest his cheek against mine.

Years later, I painted an oil portrait of my dad from a photograph I really loved. It wasn't a bad representation of him, but it wasn't quite right either. I was told to hold it up to a mirror. Amazing. In the mirror, he looked like another man. That showed me I didn't have a true perspective of him. Because I hadn't studied him from all angles, I couldn't paint my dad as he really was.

Still-life artists consider perspective to be a cornerstone of composition. A realistic painting must go beyond the two dimensions of a sketch—length and width—and represent a third dimension—depth. In a portrait, the use of perspective helps the artist to create the furrows in a person's brow, the differing planes of the face. In a still life, perspective makes flowers look like they've just been cut and those pears look appetizingly real.

In life, perspective is what gives us depth of insight. Now that I'm a grown woman with a better view of the big picture, I see many aspects of my childhood differently—including my father. I loved that time of my life when I could ride the toes of his shoes, safe and secure in his leading. But now I realize that all was not as rosy as it seemed then. My father suffered from severe depression and personal business difficulties that brought much heartache to himself and the family.

Time has brought me a broader perspective and has enabled me to see my dad in an honest light. But it hasn't changed the truth about the father I knew while I danced on his shoes. It has merely enlarged it, enabling me to see him in a more comprehensive way.

❧

In our own examination of who we are, time is a great purveyor of perspective. But time is not all we need to be able to construct a healthy, honest, well-composed life. We also need to find mirrors, like I used for my dad's portrait, that will reflect the truth about our lives. Our families and close friends are mirrors, if we're gutsy enough to ask them to point out our strengths *and* weaknesses. We can be a mirror to ourselves, if we're ready to delve deeply into our hearts, minds, and motives.

But our best mirror is God. As we've invited His company in our times of solitude, and involved Him in all the other spaces of our lives, we learn more about Him and about ourselves. We get a clear reflection of who we are because of who He is. The more we know Him, the more we can see ourselves, our lives, our families, from His perspective.

One of the benefits of seeing ourselves through His eyes is that we always get the truth. We find out that we're unique, precious women, with gifts and talents and so much to offer. We find that while we can learn from others, we don't need to compare ourselves to them.

If I watched a Martha Stewart program about Thanksgiving at her house, I would learn some valuable tips and maybe even be inspired to go back to baking my own pies. But I might also evaluate my dinner in light of hers. And, trust me, mine would always fall short.

God's perspective substitutes my family for Martha's family and my plain old turkey for hers—the one with sage leaves tucked under the skin *in a design*. (I tried that once. It looked like I'd cooked a bird with a serious skin condition.) Because the elements are mine, created by God to reflect and complement me, they fit together and my Thanksgiving wins the contest.

Having God's perspective also determines whether our still lives can hold their own in the middle of pressures that derail others. An artist's perspective keeps her on track as her painting progresses. God's perspective keeps us on track when schedules are busy, when white space is at a premium, when we're in danger of wallowing in the ordinary, when the light is nearly indistinguishable, when simplicity is merely a word in our dictionary. With a proper perspective, we can stand anything and appreciate everything. And with it, the big picture makes sense.

⁊

We invited longtime family friends to share Thanksgiving with us this year. Our oldest children are in college, and our tables seem a little bare without them. Both families need to beef up the body count. They come the morning of, with dinner rolls and poinsettias in their arms, and Gayle and I go about that age-old ritual of overfeeding families on the holidays. We have a glorious meal (the turkey meat does in fact fall off the bones) and push away from the table a satisfied bunch.

Then it's TV football. Regardless of the match-up, shouts and groans echo throughout the house.

Whenever I hear TV football, I can see Daddy in his big green

115

chair, a tray on the ottoman in front of him. On it sits the biggest bowl of oyster stew I've ever seen, before or since. Two cans of soup in that bowl, and two cans of milk, and tiny oyster crackers floating on the surface. One tall glass of milk and a dozen saltine crackers round out the meal.

Dad's out of his suit and dressed in loafers, jeans, and a red minichecked shirt unbuttoned at the neck. He's spellbound by the game. I can picture his pipe dangling from his teeth, his short, curly hair, and his trimmed fingernails.

I think about him now as I'm clearing the table, wrapping up the leftovers, dropping bits of turkey into Homer's eager mouth. Daddy's tendency to perfectionism required that *everything* be perfect on Thanksgiving, and other days as well. Trouble was—and is—nothing's ever perfect. I don't think Dad ever quite got over that.

Our still lives will never be perfectly composed though they may feel that way for isolated moments here and there. In fact, in our efforts to create a harmonious whole—embracing light and shadow, pursuing passion, creating white space—we can get everything to *appear* perfect but end up with something deeply wrong.

Because perfection is not the same as harmony. And the pursuit of perfection may lead to something exact—but flat, lifeless. The Christian life always has been, and always will be, based on a certain amount of tension. And so is the pursuit of a tranquil heart. The object is not to clear life of any obstacles to stillness, but to learn how to take on those challenges with a new kind of grace, a new sense of balance. And to recognize that balance isn't a seesaw sitting motionless and level, but one that floats up and down under the power of harmonious forces.

How dreary the carefully ordered life that is not thrown off—and then rebalanced over and over again by God's grace.

If harmony is our goal, then perfection has no place. In fact, harmony must contain some tension. The most glorious music includes a harmony with just enough dissonance and, finally, resolution. Without this contrast, we end up with pure unison (which is nice now and then on the verses). But how rich the moment when all the parts kick in!

❧

Thanksgiving is almost over now. Everywhere I look I'm satisfied with how it went, how it came together. The dining table is a mess, but the centerpiece still looks amazingly intact, undiminished by the array of dirty dishes around it.

Earlier this morning I stood back to check out the arrangement of things, the china and silver, the carefully folded napkins. Then I noticed the center of the table was…empty. I'd forgotten to plan a centerpiece.

Scrounging around on my hands and knees in the cupboard I came upon a little footed silver tray I hadn't seen in a while. After a few quick swipes of silver polish, I piled it carefully with one small, perfect pumpkin, several oranges and pears, and one bird-of-paradise blossom from the backyard. It worked. It brought the whole table together.

Art too has a center—except perhaps in the wildest abstract forms. But the center of a still-life painting is rarely, if ever, the true center of the canvas. It is instead the "visual center"—the place where the eye naturally falls when gazing at the composition. In the world of art, architecture, and mathematics this "center" is accomplished through a rule of proportion called the "Golden Mean" or the "Divine Proportion."

Although the technicalities are over my head, I get the point. It's possible to create a work of art, a piece of music—a life—so that it has an inherently compelling composition. Within that structure is a center that will draw attention without our even knowing it.

So where is the center of our own composition?

Calculated, logical attempts to locate a center in our lives inevitably fail. Planning notebooks fail. Therapy fails. Christian books fail. Doing more or doing less is not enough. Marriage is neither the answer nor the problem. Kids can fulfill and distract us. Jobs can focus and panic us.

Even getting away to nature fails us. Remember Thoreau? He found almost perfect solitude, but the stillness wasn't enough. He made a point about simple living. Yet, in the end, he hadn't made a life. After two years, he returned to Concord.

The only lasting, workable "center" is the author of the Golden Mean Himself. God doesn't offer obvious 1-2-3 steps for us to obtain even proportions, harmony, and balance in our lives. He offers… Himself. Period. And so the question is not merely: What am I doing to create a center in my life? But rather: Where do I find that center, and consequently, what will it look like?

My eyes fell on an attractive woman at the grocery store the other day. I loved her clothes; her haircut was great; and she even had a smile on her face. But her lipstick was too dark. As I think about her now, I can't remember one detail about her outfit or exactly what her hair looked like. But I can still see that lipstick. I doubt she wanted her mouth to be the center of attention it was.

Similarly, an inexperienced painter might paint a huge gray elephant filling the center of her canvas. She might spend months on the elephant, studying its parts, rendering its massiveness. But if she puts one small cherry, bright red, in the left lower corner—this will more likely be where the eye falls.

If Christ is truly at the center of our life's composition, the eye will fall there—even if much of our daily time is taken up with work, family, and big gray elephants. The spiritual structure of our lives, the nature of our choices, the condition of our souls will draw the eye to God. And someday, when our life on earth is over and the last brush strokes are left to dry for all time, the center will still be apparent.

No matter how hard we try to nurture a tranquil soul, a still life is still *life*—in all its blessed messy wonder. Day by day, only God makes sense of the light and shadow. He imparts His passion. He spreads His glory through our ordinary lives. God culls out the excess and offers us simplicity. He shows us how to use our white time to recover our souls.

"Be still," He says, "and know that I am God."[3]

↬

The last of the serving dishes lies dripping hot on the counter, waiting for the drying towel. Ron comes in to help (where's he been the last hour?), and we stand companionably at the sink finishing the cleanup. It's been a very satisfying day with friends and family around. I wouldn't change a thing, except…

The phone rings. It's Matt calling from Denver and his Thanksgiving with my sisters. He's full of news and impressions of cousins he hasn't seen since five inches and four years ago. I hear Molly pick up the extension in her room and actually turn down her music. The cleanup is put off in favor of a four-way phone conversation—two parents, two children. Thank goodness for Alexander Graham Bell.

This one day has been a small picture of my whole life—quiet at times, harmonious, complete, with everything in its place. And scrambled at times, with napkins crumpled on empty plates, peas on the floor, and a sink piled high with the kind of china I can't put in the dishwasher.

But in the middle of it all, untouched by the clutter and chaos, I see God. He is my centerpiece, bringing the whole of my still life together.

Notes

CHAPTER ONE
ONE SMALL STONE: RELEARNING SIMPLICITY

1. Lily Owens, ed., *The Works of Henry David Thoreau* (New York: Longmeadow Press, Avenel Books, Inc., 1981), 100–101.

2. Sue Bender, *Plain and Simple* (San Francisco: HarperSanFrancisco, 1989), 141.

3. Anne Morrow Lindbergh, *Gift from the Sea* (New York: Pantheon Books, 1955), 114.

4. Dallas Willard, *The Spirit of the Disciplines* (San Francisco: Harper & Row, Publishers, 1988), 204–5.

5. Richard Foster, *Celebration of Discipline* (San Francisco: Harper & Row, Publishers, 1978), 69–70.

6. Calvin Miller, *The Table of Inwardness* (Downers Grove, Ill.: InterVarsity Press, 1984), 21.

7. D. Martyn Lloyd-Jones, *Studies in the Sermon on the Mount*, vol. 2, (Grand Rapids, Mich.: Wm. B. Eerdmans Publishing Company, 1960), 63–64.

CHAPTER TWO
WHITE TIME: CREATING MARGINS OF QUIET SPACE

1. Idea for "margins" from Richard A. Swenson, M.D., *Margin* (Colorado Springs: NavPress, 1992).

2. Henri J. M. Nouwen, *The Way of the Heart* (San Francisco: HarperSanFrancisco, 1981), 30.

3. Lindbergh, *Gift from the Sea,* 114–15.

4. By Jean-Baptiste-Siméon Chardin.

5. Lindbergh, *Gift from the Sea,* 115.

6. Miller, *The Table of Inwardness,* 26.

7. Nouwen, *The Way of the Heart,* 26–27.

8. Henri J. M. Nouwen, *Making All Things New* (San Francisco: HarperSanFrancisco, 1981), 80–81.

CHAPTER THREE
HOT PINK TREES: PAINTING LIFE WITH COLOR AND PASSION

1. Marsha Sinetar, *Elegant Choices, Healing Choices* (New York: Paulist Press, 1988), 5.

2. Exodus 28:8, 17–20.

3. John Piper, *Desiring God* (Portland, Ore.: Multnomah Press, 1986), 65.

4. Miller, *The Table of Inwardness*, 88.

5. Isaiah 49:13.

CHAPTER FOUR
A LONG NIGHT'S DANCE: EMBRACING LIGHT AND SHADOW

1. Henri J. M. Nouwen, *Out of Solitude* (Notre Dame, Ind.: Ave Maria Press, 1974), 52–53.

2. Romans 8:39.

3. 2 Corinthians 4:8–17.

4. Romans 5:3–5.

5. Alan E. Nelson, *Broken in the Right Place* (Nashville, Tenn.: Thomas Nelson Publishers, 1994), vii.

6. Ibid., 48.

7. Psalm 30:11–12.

8. Philippians 4:4, 6–7.

9. 2 Corinthians 4:6.

10. Nouwen, *Out of Solitude,* 52–53.

11. Psalm 91:1.

CHAPTER FIVE
FRECKLED APPLES: CELEBRATING THE ORDINARY

1. Miller, *The Table of Inwardness,* 84.

2. Ruth Senter, *Secrets from Ordinary Places* (Grand Rapids, Mich.: Zondervan Publishing, 1990), 11–12.

3. Brother Lawrence, *The Practice of the Presence of God* (Springdale, Penn.: Whitaker House, 1982), 20.

4. As cited in Miller, *The Table of Inwardness,* 92.

5. Ibid., 75.

CHAPTER SIX
ELEPHANT STUDIES: COMPOSING THE BIG PICTURE

1. Sir Joshua Reynolds, "Notes on the Art of Painting" given to the Royal Academy in 1783, quoted in Ken Howard, ed., *Art Class* (New York: Watson-Guptill Publications, 1989), 188.

2. Lindbergh, *Gift from the Sea,* 29.

3. Psalm 46:10.